A Tale of Two Sisters

By
Chris Pack

TEACH Services, Inc.
P U B L I S H I N G
www.TEACHServices.com

Copyright © 2013 TEACH Services, Inc.
ISBN-13: 978-1-4796-0000-7 (Paperback)
ISBN-13: 978-1-4796-0001-4 (ePub)
ISBN-13: 978-1-4796-0002-1 (Kindle/Mobi)

Published by

TEACH Services, Inc.
P U B L I S H I N G
www.TEACHServices.com

Krista's Story

Ultimate Despair

Krista sprawled listlessly on her sofa contemplating her life situation. Having just turned twenty, she fearfully wondered how far into her twenties she would live. Her addiction to amphetamines, coupled with her incessant chain-smoking, was taking its toll on her physical and emotional well-being. She had dropped a significant amount of weight, and her poor diet and drug use were wreaking havoc on her teeth and her health in general. Krista had recently gone to the dentist to have a crown put on, only to have it crack and break off a couple of days after the repair. The dentist was puzzled as to why Krista's teeth were so brittle, but Krista knew.

But the newest development in her health dilemma was what sent her spiraling down to this current funk. She had been treating herself for crab lice, when she was diagnosed at the health clinic with gonorrhea too! How could this be happening to her? In her mind it was the "scum of the earth" type of people who got these diseases, and now she had become one of them.

To make matters worse, in her despair and anxiety, Krista got it in her head that the crab lice were crawling on her arms, so she relentlessly clawed at the freckles on her arms until her forearms bled and then scabbed over. What was she going to do? She was so ashamed— she felt so destitute.

A Messed Up Childhood

Krista was raised in a middle-class home with her parents and two sisters. Her father was a businessman who was totally focused on climbing the ladder of success. Thus, he had little time for the family. Krista's mother was a stay-at-home mom struggling to raise three young daughters by herself. According to Krista's father, raising children was the woman's job, especially since they had only girls. In her father's way of thinking, women were not quite as valuable as men, which showed in his favorite "endearing" pet names for his daughters: the dumb broads and dizzy dames. Krista's father also had a drinking problem, and he took liberties with Krista that no father should ever take.

As Krista approached her teen years, she hooked up with a group of friends who accepted her for who she was and gladly included her in their activities. This became the close family she longed for. She and her friends soon began to experiment with drinking and smoking, and by the age of thirteen, they were indulging in marijuana.

Fooling Around in High School

As she entered high school, she and her friends progressed to hallucinogenic drugs (LSD and mescaline). While tripping on drugs, she could totally forget everything and laugh again—everything seemed to be so funny when under the influence—but the effect didn't last long enough to really take away the problems.

Then one day when Krista thought life couldn't get worse, it did. Krista was devastated when she came home from school and found out that her family was moving again! Her father was getting promoted, and she would have to be uprooted from all her friends so her father could continue to "climb that ladder."

Krista started her sophomore year in Ventura, California, but she was extremely unhappy. Every week she earned money by ironing for her mother so that she could pay for bus fare to Santa Maria for the weekend. All would be right with the world for a few days while staying with her best friend Barbie and her family, but Sunday always came, and she dreaded going back home. Krista became so distraught with the new living situation that she attempted suicide. Her parents spoke with a minister who lived up the street from them, and based on his counsel, they decided it would be better to let Krista move back to Santa Maria and live with Barbie's family.

Krista was so elated when she heard the news; now she would be back with her friends. And the living arrangements at Barbie's house were ideal for a rebellious teenager. Barbie's mom was not as strict as Krista's mom, so the two girls pretty much did what they wanted. Barbie's mom worked full time, which also gave them more freedom to be on their own. It wasn't unusual for Barbie and Krista to go cruising with friends after school and smoke a few joints before going home. Ah, life was good once again!

But Krista's false sense of joy was jolted when, in the early winter of her junior year, she contracted hepatitis A at a party she was attending. One rather intoxicated fellow had been roaming around taking hits off of everyone's cigarettes and drinking out of whatever open beer can he could find, and no one knew he was sick. Krista had never heard of hepatitis, but one of her friends noticed yellow in the whites of Krista's eyes and asked her if she had hepatitis. After testing positive, she had to move back home with her parents for a couple of months while she recovered. Barbie's mom was pregnant, so Krista had to leave so as not to expose her to the disease.

After Krista recovered from the hepatitis, she moved back to Santa Maria. Not long after coming back, Krista met and began dating Jack. He had just moved to Santa Maria because his parents wanted him to get away from his drug-addict friends. Jack was a heroin addict and had been in a lot of trouble. His parents hoped he would make a change for the better in new surroundings, so Jack's mother moved to Santa Maria with him and rented a temporary apartment. Jack's father, who still lived in Bakersfield, came to Santa Maria on the weekends to visit. Jack's parents were alcoholics, but they were not mean like Krista's father. In fact, there were many times when Krista would hang out with Jack's mother and they would get drunk together. Krista and Jack dated all that summer before her senior year, and they were still together when school began in the fall.

When Krista showed up for school, she found out that the new computer system had messed up her class schedule. The school had her registered for classes she had already taken or did not want to take. To deal with this problem, she just quit going to school and hung out with Jack. Of course, she didn't get away with that for too long. The school contacted Barbie's mom about Krista's absences, so Krista had to go see the school counselor. Since nothing could be done about her classes and the mix-up, Krista opted to attend continuation school. This option allowed her to attend school for half the day, work at her own speed, and, best of all, smoke. One of Krista's good friends who had become pregnant was going there too, so the arrangement suited Krista just fine!

When Krista began attending continuation school, she and Barbie sort of drifted apart. They were no longer going to the same school, and Krista spent a lot of her time with Jack. Krista did not have many credits left to earn before she could graduate, so she worked hard and finished her requirements by December of her senior year. Her main motivation, of course, was so she could spend more time with Jack. Krista was not eighteen when she graduated, so she had to move back home with her family for a few months.

Jack visited her in Ventura, and she visited him, but as soon as she turned eighteen, she moved to Bakersfield with Jack and his family. Jack's family had moved back to Bakersfield after things did not work out well in Santa Maria.

Bad Influences and Good Examples

Shortly after moving to Bakersfield, Krista found a job at a car seat factory. On the first day of work, Jack drove Krista to the factory in her old 1965 Volkswagen bug and dropped her off. After leaving Krista at work, Jack hooked up with one of his old druggie buddies. They then proceeded to commit an armed robbery at a liquor store in town in

Krista's car. Of course using Krista's vintage Volkswagen bug as a get-away car was not the brightest of ideas. It wasn't hard to track the car down, and both Jack and his accomplice were promptly arrested and thrown in jail.

Krista continued to live with Jack's parents and visit Jack each weekend with them at the jail. But after a few months she decided to move into an apartment a coworker had told her about. The move was prompted by the fact that Jack's parents had moved into a condo and she was sharing a bedroom with Jack's older brother. She worked nights by this time, and his brother worked days, but she still wanted more space. She especially wanted to keep hidden the fact that she had started using drugs (amphetamines) again, and she did not need any-one poking around in her stuff!

When Jack was released from jail about nine months later, he moved into Krista's apartment. By that time though, Krista had changed, and Jack hadn't. After being knocked around a few times by Jack, Krista decided she'd had enough. She was sick and tired of the abusive relationship she had endured with him. He never kept a job and was always stealing from her, so she kicked him out of her apart-ment and out of her life for good!

Kicking Jack out didn't help the direction of her life. Instead, she had found herself in several unhealthy relationships with men who really did not care about her. Now she lay on the sofa feeling ashamed and frightened. She could not believe how disgusting she had become. With her black scabbed, emaciated arms, lifeless eyes and gaunt, dis-eased body, she thought she was just going to die.

Krista's dismal thoughts were interrupted by a faint knock on the door. When she rose to answer it, she was pleasantly surprised to find her sister, Anna, standing there. A few inches shorter than Krista, with a slight build and long dark wavy hair, Anna cautiously entered the apartment. In her hand was a small paper bag. Anna set the pa-per bag on the kitchen table and proceeded to pull out a deliciously fragrant bowl of homemade spilt pea soup and a freshly baked carrot muffin. The aroma was exquisite! Anna offered the soup and muffin to Krista, stating that she had made it that morning and thought maybe she would like some. Krista could not remember ever having anything that tasted so good! She relished every bite and scraped the soup bowl clean. It was the most nutritious meal Krista had had in a long time. Anna was amazed at how well her meager offering was received and wished that she had brought more.

Once Krista finished eating, Anna timidly asked her sister if she would come to her baptism the following weekend. Anna had recently renewed her commitment to Christ and wanted to share her new life with Krista. Krista agreed to come to the baptism, and Anna informed her of when and where it would be.

The Friday night before Anna's baptism Krista didn't sleep at all, but she still managed to arrive on time at Anna's church on Saturday morning. Despite being dressed in an extremely short mini skirt, sporting dark circles under her glassy eyes, and emitting the pungent odor of a well-used ashtray, Krista was received warmly as she entered the church. Anna met Krista at the door, and as Krista signed the guest book, Anna introduced her to Lila, the Bible worker who had been studying with her. Lila was very bubbly with bright shining eyes—she seemed to glow with happiness. Krista thought to herself, What a nice lady.

Next, Anna led Krista to the Bible study class that met each week before church. Krista felt rather helpless not knowing anything about the Bible, but she tried to comprehend what the class was studying about as best she could. Anna shared her Bible with Krista to try to help her follow along.

Once the class ended, Anna left to get ready for the baptism, so Lila escorted Krista to a center seat where she would be able to easily see the baptismal tank. Settling in on the brown padded pew, she gazed about at her surroundings. Krista had not been to a church since she was a small child, and she had never seen a baptism by emersion before. She was curious about the big tank of water with the see-through glass centered above the platform of the church. She was intensely focused as her sister and the minister made their way down the steps of the baptismal tank into the water clad in their flowing robes. The minister spoke some about Anna's journey in finding Christ, but the one thing that stuck out in Krista's mind most was when the minister laid Anna back into the watery grave and then she burst back up out of the water to her new life in Christ. At that very moment Krista knew that this was the way she wanted to go. Something inside her spoke strongly to this effect, and for the first time in a long time, she had hope.

After the church service, Krista and Anna went outside. Since arriving at church two hours ago, Krista had not had a cigarette, so she asked Anna if it would be alright to smoke outside the church. Anna did not think that would be such a good idea, so they said their good-byes, and Krista headed home.

When Krista arrived home, her live-in boyfriend Eric was there. She told him about the service, but he did not seem that interested. Krista had a lot to ponder though since she wanted to follow the same path her sister had found, but she did not know how.

Anna had been living with an elderly lady who Lila knew. But shortly after her baptism, Lila mentioned to Anna that she had a good friend who had just been re-baptized and was living in St. Helena, California. Lila thought it might be a good idea for Anna to move up there with her friend Greta, so they could encourage each other. Besides, Anna needed to get away from the environment she was in, and there was a lovely Christian college near Greta's home. So Anna packed up her Volkswagen bug and headed to St. Helena. Krista was extremely sad to see her sister go, but she was happy for her too, wishing she could be going with her.

Krista, in the meantime, had been trying to read her Bible, but she wasn't getting very far. She also was struggling with trying to quit smoking and doing drugs since she felt that she would not be accepted by God if she continued these habits, but she was failing terribly.

A Turning Point

Not long after Anna moved, Krista received a letter from her. Anna had been studying the Bible with another Bible worker, and she shared with Krista what she had been learning. A Bible verse that Anna quoted in the letter was exactly what Krista needed to hear. The text said, "If we confess our sins, He is faithful and just to forgive us our sins and to cleanse us from all unrighteousness" (1 John 1:9). Krista read the text several times and let it sink in for a few minutes. This was a totally new concept to her, but when the concept finally penetrated her mind, she was extremely excited! It was God who would do the cleaning up in her life. Right then and there she told God that she wanted to do whatever He wanted her to do.

That evening Krista went to work as usual. She smoked during all the breaks and took her normal hit of speed. But when she got home that morning, something unusual happened. She went to light up a cigarette, but it tasted awful. So she got a new pack out of her carton, but that one tasted terrible too. Then an almost audible thought came to her mind as if Someone was reminding her of something she wanted to do: Well, you wanted to quit smoking anyway. It was as if a light came on, and she thought, Oh yeah! That was the last cigarette Krista ever smoked.

A few minutes later Krista heard a knock on her door. It was her next-door neighbor, Sandy, who worked at the factory with her. Sandy knew Krista always had cigarettes, so she had come over to buy a pack from her. Sandy could hardly comprehend Krista's reply when Krista told her that she had quit smoking and that Sandy could have the rest of the carton. Krista then slid open the coffee table drawer where she kept her amphetamines and said, "Here you can have the rest of my speed too." Sandy's big brown eyes grew as large as saucers when Krista's words sank into her consciousness. Sandy and Krista had been partying buddies for quite awhile, and she was totally shocked at this sudden change. Sandy took the cigarettes and drugs and slowly backed out of Krista's apartment door, staring at Krista the whole time in wide-eyed disbelief. Sandy gently closed the door, but then opened it again slightly and peeked in at Krista one more time with that same wide-eyed gaze. Something strange, that she did not understand, was definitely happening in Krista's life.

A few days later, after Krista had gotten home from work, there was a knock at the door. Krista was surprised and delighted to see Lila, the Bible worker who had studied with Anna. Lila had stopped by because she had some mail that had come to her address for Anna. It was all junk mail, but it was a divine appointment set up by God. After some small talk, Krista asked Lila if she could have Bible studies. Of course, Lila's shining eyes lit up, and she replied that she would love to study with her. Lila gave Krista a set of lessons to start studying, and they set a time for the next week to go over them.

Krista was elated about starting the studies, but something inside was troubling her. Since the morning she had told God she wanted to follow Him, she had not spent much time with Eric. She somehow knew that Eric living there was not right, so she got some boxes and packed up his things. When he got home that evening, Krista told him that he needed to move out. Eric did not protest at all. He just loaded up his things and left, which was another gift from God.

When Don, the drug dealer Krista used to get her speed from, found out that she had quit using the drug, he was astounded. So one day, out of the blue, Don brought a man whom Krista had never met before to her apartment. The man was sort of rough looking with lots of tattoos, chains, and a leather vest. When the man was seated on the couch, Don said, "This is Krista. She used to do more speed than even I can do, and she smoked like a freight train. Now look at her, she has quit everything!"

Krista was sort of taken aback by what Don said. She felt as if she was some sort of freak show that Don had brought Bruce, his friend, to see. But what came next was even more amazing. Bruce, with his seemingly tough exterior, after thinking about what Don had said, looked straight into Krista's eyes and asked, "How did you do it?" Krista was so overjoyed to be able to share with him how the power of God had changed her life. After they talked for awhile, Don and Bruce left. She never saw Bruce again, but it was not the last she would see of Don.

Krista continued her Bible studies with Lila and was enjoying them so much. Each week she learned something new. One day Lila introduced Krista to the health message. Krista had gone out of town deep sea fishing the previous week and brought back some fish, which she had in her freezer. After she and Lila's study, she tried to give Lila some of the fish to take home. Lila informed Krista that she did not eat meat of any kind. Krista had never thought of fish as meat before. She had a childhood friend who belonged to a certain church that did not eat meat on Friday, but they ate fish. Lila went on to tell Krista how at one Bible study she was giving there were two small children passing a chicken wing back and forth to each other. As she observed them, all she could think about was the chicken flapping its wing. That scenario struck Krista like a bolt of lightening. She had never associated eating meat with the dead animal.

That evening Krista was called into work early. Krista took the frozen fish out of the freezer and tried to fry it. But the more she repeatedly stabbed at it with the spatula to thaw it out, the more grossed out she became. She did finally eat the fish for dinner, but that was the last time she ever ate any kind of meat again. She later found out why God took that desire from her as she came to understand the health benefits of the original diet that God gave to Adam and Eve in the Garden of Eden of nuts, fruits, grains, and vegetables.

The more Krista studied, the better she began to comprehend God's law of love and His tremendous love for her. She saw that the

Ten Commandments were not restrictions, but more like a safety net to steer her around the pitfalls of this world. She was so thankful to finally have some guidelines on how to live. She also came to realize that the seventh day Sabbath was the true Sabbath and that God had never changed it. She found that the Sabbath was a blessing, as it allowed time to be with family and friends at church and at home. It was also a time to get out in nature and enjoy the beauty of God's creation. But best of all it was a time to learn more about Jesus and fellowship with Him.

Krista also learned, as she grew in her relationship with God, that Jesus loves for His children to take time to talk to Him and get to know Him through the Bible. It makes Him so happy when His children want to be with Him, just like an earthly father or mother loves their children and wants to be with them. The wonderful thing about God's love though is that it is constant—there is nothing we can do that will make Him love us less. He takes us just as we are, and as we behold His great love for us, we are changed to be like Him through the power of the Holy Spirit.

Krista continued to study with Lila, and then one day she felt ready to publicly profess her new faith in God through baptism. Plans were made for the ceremony, and Krista eagerly looked forward to the Sabbath when she would begin her new life as a precious child of God.

Krista had been invited to Lila's apartment for dinner the Friday evening before her baptism to discuss the details of the worship service. As she was getting ready to leave, she received a phone call from work telling her that she needed to come in to work that evening at eleven o'clock. When she got to Lila's place, she told her about the phone call. This was the first time that Krista would have to stand up for her new beliefs. Lila had her call the factory, and she coached Krista on what to say. When Krista was asked why she was not coming in, she replied that it was because of her religious convictions, which was a new term in her vocabulary. She explained that she kept the Sabbath now from sundown Friday to sundown Saturday. Gladly, her boss seemed satisfied with that answer.

Krista enjoyed the rest of the evening as she and Lila reviewed her baptismal vows and discussed the biblical reasons behind each one. She was learning so much, and it was all so good! Lila also suggested that she call her parents and invite them to her baptism, since they did not live too far away. Krista got up the courage to make the call only to be disappointed by their answer; of course, she was not surprised, for they had refused to come to Anna's baptism also.

After arriving home from Lila's that evening, there was a knock on her door. Standing in the doorway was Don, and she let him come in. He looked pitiful, and as soon as they were seated on the couch, he started giving her a sob story about his ex-wife and not getting to see his daughter. Krista felt sorry for him and was trying to comfort him when he started kissing her on the neck. He was a big man, but Krista managed to push him away. Unfortunately, it was not before he had left a couple of red marks on her neck. Krista told Don that he had to leave and he did, but the damage had already been done. When she looked in the mirror she was aghast at what she saw. How could she get baptized the next day with horrid red marks on her neck. Krista tore through her closet searching for a dress with a high collar. It was the middle of summer in the scorching hot, desert town where she lived, but she was determined to wear her high collared dress with the long sleeves the next day so that she could look proper for her baptism!

The next morning Krista was joyful as she climbed out of bed and got ready for church. When she looked in the mirror though, she was reminded of the fiasco she had endured the evening before. She applied makeup the best she could to try to cover the hideous spots, threw on her high collared, long-sleeved dress and headed for church, trying to ignore the roasting heat of that hot July day. When she arrived, she was very self-conscious about the marks and kept fiddling with the collar of her dress. No one seemed to notice though, and if they did, at least nothing was said. Krista was relieved.

When it was time for her baptism, Krista descended the same steps Anna had just a few months before. It was like a dream come true how the turn of events had come about. The minister spoke to the congregation about the blessing of a new life in Christ. Then Krista was submerged into the baptismal waters. As she came back up, she felt a joy she had never known before! She was so very thankful to be a child in the family of God!

Not long after her baptism, Krista, her parents, and her younger sister, Janie, went up to Northern California to visit Anna. Anna had decided to enroll at Pacific Union College, the Christian college near Greta's home. As they surveyed the beautifully designed campus perched on a mountaintop, surrounded by evergreens and gorgeous blooming flowers, Krista found herself drawn to the idea of maybe going to school there too. Anna had taken some college classes in the past, but Krista had never even thought about going to college. As they stood by a railing scanning the breathtaking view, Krista worked up the nerve to ask her parents if she could go to college there also. Krista was not prepared for her parents' response—they were extremely enthusiastic about the idea. Krista's mother was especially happy as she had worried about Krista and the environment she had been living in. And for her father, it looked better if his daughters were at least college educated. So it was settled; they would both start college in the fall.

On Krista's first night back at work after visiting Anna, she let her supervisor know that she would be quitting soon. He said he was disappointed since they had been considering her for one of the shift supervisor positions. That was quite a compliment, and Krista was taken off guard when he mentioned it. For a fleeting moment she thought about it, but then replied firmly, "No, I am going to college in Northern California."

Looking back on the job offer later, she decided that maybe the devil didn't want her going to a Christian college and tried to tempt her to stay in that environment, in the same way he had tried to stop her from getting baptized by having Don come over the night before. She was so thankful to see how God had overruled and given her the strength and determination to follow His leading.

Before long Krista was living in the dorm with Anna and attending Pacific Union College. God had fulfilled the desires of her heart more wonderfully than she could have ever imagined!

Anna's Story

A Rough Beginning

Anna was the oldest of the three girls in her family. Her mother was an only child, and she had not been around children much, so motherhood was extremely difficult for her. As a baby Anna had been very colicky, and her crying threw her father into fits of rage. At night if she was crying in her crib, instead of comforting her, her father would go into her room and scream at her to "shut up!" Her mother felt bad about this, but she lived in fear of her husband during those days, and as a new mother, she did not know what to do either.

Subsequently, Anna grew up to be a nervous, timid, and very fearful child. If she wanted to ask her mother a question, she would follow her around and try to work up the courage to do so. Her father got very angry with this behavior. One day when she was about nine years old she was following her mother around, and her father noticed and screamed, "What's the matter with you? Are you pregnant or something?" Poor Anna; she hardly even knew what that meant, and yet she was being accused of it.

Around the ages of seven and five, Anna and Krista had long hair that was very difficult for their mother to manage. To deal with the problem, their mother sat them down on a stool on the back patio and gave both of them a haircut. The girls thought it was wonderfully exciting to have shorter hair. Plus their mother had bought them both sailor hats to wear. They thought it was so fascinating to flip the sailor hat brim up and down, and they were having lots of fun doing so. Later that evening when their father got home they ran to show him their new hairdos and hats. But when their father saw them, his face turned crimson red. He flew into a rage and punched the sliding glass door so hard that the girls ran in fear as he yelled and cursed at their mother for cutting their hair. Evidently girls were supposed to have long hair according to his rules.

A Means of Escape

Anna, like Krista, found great comfort in her group of friends, and she turned to them on many occasions. One evening while the family was eating dinner, Anna, who was in seventh grade at that time, accidentally spilled some of her food. She didn't mean to, but she got nervous a lot and tended to spill things, especially when around her father. Anna's father was so irate about her spilling her food that he took off his belt and started swinging it wildly at Anna. She ran to her bedroom and had to jump back and forth between the two single beds in the room in an attempt to dodge the lashing. After her father's tantrum died down, he left the room. Anna took that opportunity to make her escape. She jumped out of her bedroom window and ran a couple of houses down the street to her best friend Sherry's home. She stayed the night with her, knowing that she would be safe there.

When the family moved to Santa Maria, Anna was a freshman in high school. She too got into the partying scene—drinking, smoking, and eventually drugs. She had a big group of friends and was hardly ever home. She never enjoyed school much, and by the end of her sophomore year, she had had enough of school.

After the first couple of weeks of her junior year, Anna dropped out of high school. She and a friend of hers were transferred to continuation high school, but at the time it was not very well organized. Anna and her friend, Carol, would sign into school and then leave. They would then drive around town and smoke pot the rest of the day. Anna, at that time, also had an alcoholic boyfriend who she spent time with. Some days he would come to her house at lunch with his quart of Coors beer and sit at the kitchen table and drink. Then he would go back to work at the record store. After he lost his job at the record store and his driver's license, he got around town on his bike. Sadly, you would see him with a six-pack of beer on the back rack of the bike. Needless to say, Anna's mother was relieved when that relationship ended.

At the beginning of Anna's senior year, her father brought an elderly man to the house to meet Anna. The man had an airplane, and her father was trying to get Anna and some of her friends to fly with him to San Francisco to a rock concert. During the meeting the elderly man took some pictures out of his wallet and showed her father. They both were grinning and lusting after the pictures, so Anna figured they must be pictures of indecent women, which made her very uncomfortable.

The next day after this meeting they invited Anna to meet them at a Denny's restaurant for lunch. When Anna met with them, she again experienced those same uneasy feelings, so she told them she had had enough, and she walked out. She was so disgusted by it all. She could not understand why her father had introduced her to this creepy, strange person.

She decided then and there to run away. She went to a friend's house and had him drive her to the bus station. Then she instructed him to take her car to another friend's house and leave it there. Anna breathed a sigh of relief as she boarded the bus. This would be a welcome escape. She headed to Los Angeles first. From there she contacted her old friend Sherry who was supposed to go to a night class that evening, so she was able to get out of the house to pick her up from the bus station. Sherry then took Anna over to another friend's house whose parents were on vacation for a couple of weeks. After being gone about a week and a half, Anna called her friend Candice in Santa Maria to let her know where she was and that she was okay. Unfortunately, Candice's mother, who was also Anna's father's secretary, answered the phone, and Anna was busted!

After this episode Anna was given a home tutor to help her finish up high school. During this time she isolated herself from her friends and became very depressed. She had never been one to eat much and had always been a very finicky eater. Since she was at home now most of the time, she started trying out the different junk foods that she had really never noticed before. Anna switched her drug addiction to a food addiction. When this happened, the one friend she did have, Pete, had a hard time figuring out what had happened to Anna. She went from an aggressive, in-your-face type of person to a shy, withdrawn girl with a mild disposition. But having Pete around was not the best influence for Anna as he had a mental illness and just made things more confusing and depressing.

Near the end of Anna's senior year her family got the news that her father was being transferred to Ventura. The move left her even more depressed and lonely. She had also been gaining weight, which she had never done before. Krista was not there much, because she visited her friends in Santa Maria every weekend, and her other sister, Janie, being six years younger than Anna, did not have much in common with her. Anna was in a very bad place emotionally.

Engaging With the Devil

One day Anna was flipping channels trying to find something to watch on the television, when she came across a religious program. It was a Billy Graham crusade, and she sat captivated as she listened to the message. At the end of the program, she gave her life to God. Right away she began attending a non-denominational church that was not too far from their home. Anna's mother had been attending that church, so Anna joined her.

Still, things were not going that great, and one afternoon everything just seemed to come to a head. Anna was still very depressed and had stuffed a lot of anger about a lot of things for a long time deep inside her. One day while sitting in the upstairs TV room of their home, she suddenly exploded. She broke the lamp and totally trashed the room in a fit of rage and despair. Anna's mother did not know what to do and asked the pastor of her church for advice. Pastor Paul agreed to help, so Anna began going to him for counseling.

Anna was soon invited to come to their monthly "healing" group that met at the pastor's home. Arlene, Paul's wife, would lie on the floor, and everyone would form a circle around her. The room would be dark with very cold drafts of air rushing by their feet. Paul would go around behind each person and lay his hands on them and pray. Then they would wait to see if there was a message for that person from "the other side." If there was a message, a low gravelly male voice would begin talking through Arlene to that person. These were supposedly departed loved ones who wanted to make contact with living friends and relatives. These voices were not departed loved ones, though, but actually voices of demons.

The Bible teaches in Ecclesiastes 9:5, 6, and 10 that "the living know that they will die, but the dead know nothing, and they have no more reward. For the memory of them is forgotten. Also their love, their hatred and their envy have now perished; nevermore will they have a share in anything done under the sun … for there is no work or device or knowledge or wisdom in the grave where you are going." But this church did not follow the Bible, and so it was left wide open for whatever deception Satan and the evil angels could devise.

After being in Ventura for about a year, Pastor Paul informed her of a summer missionary opportunity in Philadelphia, Pennsylvania, working with underprivileged children. Anna signed on for the job, but when she returned home at the end of the summer, she was extremely thin. She had lost all the weight she had gained and then some. When she went to visit Krista and Barbie in Santa Maria, they got scared when they could see the detail of every rib protruding from her sides as she undressed for bed—she looked like a walking skeleton. At that time eating disorders were nonexistent, as far as the public knew, but later in life Anna was diagnosed with anorexia.

For the next three to four years Anna continued going to the church and her group. Arlene, the pastor's wife who was the medium, found that the demons were beginning to have increasing control over her and were becoming more demanding of her time. Paul and Arlene had studied with Edward Cayce and also were followers of Jean Dixon. They had, thus, been led astray, thinking that the power of the devil was the power of God.

One day Anna ran into one of the former members of the group at a store, and she asked her why she had stopped attending the meetings. The woman replied that she had begun to hear voices telling her to do terrible things. She felt it had something to do with going to the group, so she had quit coming. Anna pondered this new piece of information.

Beginning to feel restless and ready for a change, Anna dropped out of the college classes she was taking and decided to move to Bakersfield and see what her sister Krista was up to. She moved in with Krista for a couple of weeks until she found a job. Then when she saved enough money, she rented an apartment. At first she worked at a gas station, but then she found a job at the factory next to the one where Krista worked.

A Twisted Relationship

One afternoon while getting ready to leave work a male worker from the next shift approached Anna and began talking with her. He was of African American descent, of average height, and about twenty years her senior. His name was Frank, and he told Anna that he was separated from his wife and living in a hotel. Frank was a very smooth manipulator, and he eventually managed to move from the hotel, to sleeping in his car at Anna's apartment parking lot, to moving into Anna's apartment. Anna was not particularly attracted to Frank, but he seemed to have some kind of control over her. He had told Anna that God had impressed him that he would meet a woman who did not shave her arms or legs and that she would be his soul mate. Anna was not shaving at the time, and Frank did not know that, so this contributed to her thinking that maybe Frank was sent to her from God.

During their discussions Anna told Frank about her healing group that she used to go to at her former pastor's home. Frank's wife was a Seventh-day Adventist, and he knew from her and his upbringing by Seventh-day Baptist parents that what Anna had been involved in was not from God. Frank gave Anna a magazine one day with Jean Dixon's picture on the front. Anna, thinking that is was a positive article about spiritualism, flipped through the magazine to find the article. When she realized that the article was speaking against what she believed, she became notably upset and threw the magazine across the room. But the Holy Spirit was working with Anna, and suddenly a light came on in her mind, giving her understanding of the truth that the dead know nothing and that they do not communicate with the living. She also learned that it is the devil and the fallen angels that are able to impersonate the dead.

As time went by, Frank asked Anna if she loved him. Anna was honest with him and said that she wasn't sure. Frank then pulled a knife, held it to her throat, and demanded she say she loved him. Out of shock and fear, she told him she did. Frank then lied to Anna and told her that he had been in juvenile hall from age thirteen to eighteen for trying to kill his girlfriend who had tried to break up with him. At first Anna rebelled against Frank's controlling ways, but eventually he broke down her fighting spirit by the repeated threats. She began telling him she loved him without having the knife put to her throat, and she tried to please him the best she could.

One thing Frank kept insisting on was that Anna get baptized and keep the seventh day Sabbath if she was going to be a Christian. Anna believed Frank because he seemed to know a lot more about the Bible than she did. When she questioned him about his wife and eight children, Frank lied and told her that the Bible said it is alright to have two wives. Anna believed him as she did not know any better.

One Saturday morning Frank took Anna to a Seventh-day Adventist church; of course, it was not the one his wife and children attended.

Anna and Frank were greeted by Lila, the Bible worker, and asked to sign the guest book. Anna told Lila that she wanted to be baptized, but Lila told her they needed to study the Bible first to know what it taught about God so she would be grounded in truth. Anna requested Bible studies, so Lila began coming to the apartment. But each time Lila came Frank would hide, often taking up residence in the bathroom while she was there.

Frank had begun to trust Anna more since she was being so submissive, so he decided to go visit his parents one weekend without Anna. That Saturday morning Anna got up and went to church by herself. When she saw Lila, Lila asked Anna where her friend was. Anna told Lila that he was visiting relatives and that he was separated from his Seventh-day Adventist wife. Lila checked into the other churches around town to see what she could find out about Frank. Frank's wife knew that he was living with Anna, and Lila found out about the details of their situation.

At the next Bible study, Frank was not home, and Lila informed Anna that living together without being married goes against what the Bible teaches. She also helped Anna understand that you cannot be married to two wives. Anna truly wanted to follow whatever God wanted her to do. Lila then explained to Anna that she would have to tell Frank to leave. Lila did not know all that was going on with Frank and how controlling he was or that he was an alcoholic. Lila also did not know that Frank had threatened to kill Anna if she tried to end things with him. But Anna was too timid to tell Lila all of this.

After Lila left, Anna proceeded to pack up all of Frank's things. She also took all the knives and hid them in the refrigerator drawer under some food. Upon Frank's arrival home, Anna told him what Lila had said and that he needed to move out. To Anna's amazement, Frank just loaded up his car and left. But things were not going to be that easy!

Around three o'clock in the morning Anna was awakened by someone trying to break into her apartment. Frank was pulling the air conditioner out of the window. Anna did not have a phone, so she could not call for help. When Frank finally managed to get in, he set his half consumed whiskey bottle on the counter. Next he began searching for the kitchen knives—he even looked in the refrigerator drawer, but he did not see them. Anna giggled slightly at the fact he could not find the knives, which just enraged him more. He was so angry that he started beating on her and cursing, while telling her he was going to kill her. He then began choking her with his hands, but he could not get a tight enough grip. So he took off his belt, looped it around Anna's neck, and started choking her with it, while dragging her across the floor by her neck. Anna desperately tried to get her fingers between the belt and her throat, but she couldn't. She thought to herself, at least if I die, I am doing the right thing. In that moment the twenty-third Psalm came to her mind, the part which says, "Yea, though I walk through the valley of the shadow of death, I will fear no evil; For You are with me." Just as she was about to lose consciousness, the belt broke, and Frank passed out.

Anna lay on the floor in a crumpled heap for about two hours, afraid to move. When she finally managed to get up, she took the bottle of whiskey and dumped most of it out. She was in too much shock to do much more, so she just sat there until Frank woke up. When he saw that she had dumped out most of his whiskey, he was irate, but miracle of miracles, he got up and walked out the door!

After Frank left that morning, Anna called Krista from a pay phone to see if she would take her to get some boxes for packing since her car was not running well. Anna's call woke Krista up, but she grumpily agreed to come over. She took Anna to get the boxes, but Anna never said a word about her situation. So Krista went back home and Anna began packing boxes.

While Anna was packing, Frank showed up. He was extremely repentant for all that had happened, and he asked Anna if she would reconsider leaving. Anna considered staying, but she had to go meet

Lila that evening, so she did not give him a response.

Heading in a New Direction

Originally Anna was supposed to be baptized that evening at the church prayer meeting, but when Anna met up with Lila at the church that night, she asked if it would be alright to wait until the following Sabbath because she wanted Krista to be there. By the providence of God, Anna ended up staying the night with Lila.

In the morning while Lila was fixing her hair, Anna stood in the bathroom doorway talking to her. As they were conversing, Lila noticed the marks on Anna's neck. When Anna relayed to Lila what had happened, Lila was very adamant that Anna was not to go back to her apartment alone and that she needed to get out of there that day! Lila then contacted a young single mother from the church and asked her if she would go with Anna to finish packing and cleaning the apartment. Then Lila spoke with an elderly member from the church and asked if it would be alright for Anna to stay with her for a little while, and the lady agreed to have her come.

The following weekend Anna was baptized, and she soon moved to Northern California to live with Greta, Lila's friend.

Epilogue

Anna and her husband are in the Philippines, where he serves as director of the Theology Department at the Adventist university. Throughout their marriage, they have served the church in ministry, he as a pastor leading a congregation and Anna as a pastor's wife assisting in a variety of areas, including teaching children's Sabbath School classes.

When Anna's son and daughter began school, Anna went back to college and graduated from Loma Linda University with an associate's degree in occupational therapy.

Krista and her husband are involved in church ministries. Her husband is prison ministries leader for their church, and Krista helps with providing food for special events. Recently they have been delivering Bible studies to help promote an upcoming evangelistic series.

Krista went back to college after her two daughters started school in 1989, and she graduated with an associate's degree in physical therapy in 1992 from Greenville Tech in Greenville, South Carolina.

Dear reader, God loves you, and it is Anna and Krista's hope that through their story you will behold His love and power that gives peace and freedom through knowing Him. No matter how low we have fallen He is there to pick us up, dust us off, and set us on the right path. In Proverbs 3:5 and 6 it says, "Trust in the Lord with all your heart, and lean not on your own understanding; In all your ways acknowledge Him, and He shall direct your paths." Thanks and praise be to our loving God! May we daily seek a deeper relationship with the Lord and be ready for His return.

We invite you to view the complete
selection of titles we publish at:

www.TEACHServices.com

Scan with your mobile
device to go directly
to our website.

Please write or email us your praises, reactions, or
thoughts about this or any other book we publish at:

TEACH Services, Inc.
P U B L I S H I N G
www.TEACHServices.com

P.O. Box 954
Ringgold, GA 30736

info@TEACHServices.com

TEACH Services, Inc., titles may be purchased in bulk for
educational, business, fund-raising, or sales promotional use.
For information, please e-mail:

BulkSales@TEACHServices.com

Finally, if you are interested in seeing
your own book in print, please contact us at

publishing@TEACHServices.com

We would be happy to review your manuscript for free.

www.ingramcontent.com/pod-product-compliance
Lightning Source LLC
Chambersburg PA
CBHW060918050426

42453CB00010B/1800